chocolate
sensations

SB

SILVERDALE BOOKS

Published in 2001 by Silverdale Books
An Imprint of Bookmart Ltd.
Registered Number 2372865
Trading as Bookmart Limited
Desford Road
Enderby
Leicester
LE9 5AD
Copyright (c) Trident Press International 2001

acknowledgements

Chocolate Sensations
Designed & Compiled by: R&R Publications Marketing Pty. Ltd.
Creative Director: Paul Sims
Production Manager: Paul Sims
Food Photography: Warren Webb, William Meppem, Andrew Elton, Quentin Bacon, Gary Smith, Per Ericson, Paul Grater, Ray Joice, John Stewart, Ashley Mackevicius, Harm Mol, Yanto Noerianto, Andy Payne.
Food Stylists: Stephane Souvlis, Janet Lodge, Di Kirby, Wendy Berecry, Belinda Clayton, Rosemary De Santis, Carolyn Fienberg, Jacqui Hing, Michelle Gorry, Christine Sheppard, Donna Hay.

Recipe Development: Ellen Argyriou, Sheryle Eastwood, Kim Freedman, Lucy Kelly, Donna Hay, Anneka Mitchell, Penelope Peel, Jody Vassallo, Belinda Warn, Loukie Werle.
Proof Reader: Samantha Calcott

Includes Index
ISBN 1 85605 653 8
EAN 9781856056533

First Edition Printed September 2000
Computer Typeset in Humanist 521 & Times New Roman

Printed in China

contents

Ah, chocolate!

From Aztec times people have enjoyed the tastes provided by the seeds of the tropical cocoa tree, called cocoa beans, which are the source of chocolate.

Advances in processing over the years have produced a variety of wonderful products, from unsweetened cocoa drink to milk chocolate. Cocoa pods are harvested and then broken open, removing the seeds and pulp. Seeds are then fermented for a period of two to ten days, to develop flavour; they are then dried, graded, packed and shipped to all corners of the world.

Chocolate manufacturers blend seeds from various areas to obtain a consistent style and flavour. The selected seeds are cleaned and blended then roasted to further develop flavour and aroma. After roasting and cooling, seeds are shelled, saving the meat, and the unwanted shells are normally sold off for animal feed. The meat (or nibs) which are about 50 percent cocoa butter, are then ground to produce chocolate liquor. The manufacturer will then use this ingredient alone, or blended with other ingredients to make specific types of chocolate or chocolate products.

Chocolate types

Chocolate-flavoured syrup:

Basically corn syrup and cocoa with preservatives , emulsifiers, and flavourings.

Commercial coating chocolate:

Used by professional confectioners who use coating chocolate for dipping and for making curls, ruffles and other garnishes. It has more cocoa butter than regular baking chocolate which allows it to melt and spread well.

Compound chocolate coating:

This is an imitation product and does not normally contain cocoa.

Eating chocolate:

Cocoa and sugar are added to chocolate liquor. Distinctions of bittersweet, semisweet and sweet do not correspond to any fixed degree of sweetness; the amount of sugar depends on the formula of the individual manufacturer.

Milk chocolate:

Dried milk solids are added to sweetened chocolate. Widely used for chocolate bars and confectionary, but rarely used for cooking.

Powdered cocoa:

Enough cocoa is pressed out of the chocolate liquor to leave a press cake with a content of between 10 to 25 percent cocoa butter.

Instant cocoa:

Contains lecithin, an emulsifier that makes cocoa easier to dissolve in cold liquids.

Solid unsweeted chocolate:

Generally poured into moulds and solidified. Used mainly in cooking.

White chocolate:

Lacks chocolate liquor, so is technically not real chocolate. Contains cocoa butter with added sugar, milk and flavourings. May contain lecithin and usually vanilla or vanillin. Should not be substituted for chocolate in recipes.

Whatever the occasion, chocolate is a celebration all of its own!

This collection of mouth-watering cakes, puddings and desserts is guaranteed to gladden the hearts and delight the taste buds of chocolate lovers everywhere. Luscious cakes and gateaux, creamy desserts and puddings, fresh fruit combinations, feather-light souffles and chocolate box treats, all are represented here. Whether you yearn for old favourites, chocolate home-bakes, or a spectacular centrepiece for that special celebration, these recipes are sure to satisfy the longings of even the most discerning chocoholics.

choc-almond biscotti

biscuit barrel

Reach into the barrel and pull out a

lusciously rich and sumptuous chocolate treat. Temptations in this chapter cover cookies, biscuits, brownies, biscotti, blondies, and macaroons.

mocha-
truffle cookies

Photograph on right

ingredients

125g/4oz butter, chopped
90g/3oz dark chocolate, broken into pieces
2 tablespoons instant espresso coffee powder
2¹/₂ cups/315g/10oz flour
¹/₂ cup/45g/1¹/₂oz cocoa powder
1 teaspoon baking powder
2 eggs, lightly beaten
1 cup/250g/8oz sugar
1 cup/170g/5¹/₂oz brown sugar
2 teaspoons vanilla essence
125g/4oz pecans, chopped

Oven temperature 180°C, 350°F, Gas 4

Method:
1 Place butter, chocolate and coffee powder in a heatproof bowl. Set over a saucepan of simmering water and heat, stirring, until mixture is smooth. Remove bowl from pan and set aside to cool slightly.
2 Sift together flour, cocoa powder and baking powder into a bowl. Add eggs, sugar, brown sugar, vanilla essence and chocolate mixture and mix well to combine. Stir in pecans.
3 Drop tablespoons of mixture onto greased baking trays and bake for 12 minutes or until puffed. Stand cookies on trays for 2 minutes before transferring to wire racks to cool.
Note: This is the biscuit version of the traditional rich truffle confection and tastes delicious as an after-dinner treat with coffee.
Makes 40

choc
layer biscuits

Photograph on right

ingredients

250g/8oz butter
1 cup/170g/5¹/₂oz brown sugar
³/₄ cup/185g/6oz sugar
2 teaspoons vanilla essence
1 egg
2³/₄ cups/350g/11oz flour
1 teaspoon baking powder
¹/₂ cup/45g/1¹/₂oz cocoa powder
¹/₂ cup/45g/1¹/₂oz malted milk powder

Oven temperature 180°C, 350°F, Gas 4

Method:
1 Place butter, brown sugar, sugar and vanilla essence in a bowl and beat until light and fluffy. Add egg and beat well. Sift together flour and baking powder. Add flour mixture to butter mixture and mix to make a soft dough.
2 Divide dough into two equal portions. Knead cocoa powder into one portion and malted milk powder into the other.
3 Roll out each portion of dough separately on nonstick baking paper to make a 20x30cm/8x12in rectangle. Place chocolate dough on top of malt dough and press together.
4 Cut in half lengthwise and place one layer of dough on top of the other. You should now have four layers of dough in alternating colours. Place layered dough on a tray, cover with plastic food wrap and chill for 1 hour.
5 Cut dough into 1cm/¹/₂in-wide fingers and place on greased baking trays. Bake for 15 minutes or until biscuits are golden and crisp. Transfer to wire racks to cool.
Note: For a special occasion, dip the ends of cooled biscuits into melted white or dark chocolate and place on a wire rack until chocolate sets.
Makes 40

original
choc-chip cookies

Method:

1 *Place butter and sugar in a bowl and beat until light and fluffy. Beat in egg.*

2 *Add sifted flour, baking powder, coconut, chocolate chips and hazelnuts to butter mixture and mix to combine.*

3 *Drop tablespoons of mixture onto greased baking trays and bake for 12-15 minutes or until cookies are golden. Transfer to wire racks to cool.*

Note: *Everyone's favourite biscuit, it is full of the flavour of coconut, toasted hazelnuts and a generous portion of chocolate chips!*

Makes 35

ingredients

250g/8oz butter, softened
1 cup/170g/5¹/₂oz brown sugar
1 egg
2 cups/250g/6oz plain flour
1¹/₄ teaspoons baking powder
45g/1¹/₂oz desiccated coconut
220g/7oz chocolate chips
185g/6oz hazelnuts, toasted, roughly chopped

Oven temperature 180°C, 350°F, Gas 4

double-choc
brownies

Method:

1 Place sugar, chocolate, oil, vanilla essence and eggs in a bowl and whisk to combine. Sift together flour and baking powder. Add flour mixture to chocolate mixture and mix well to combine.

2 Pour mixture into a greased and lined 20cm/8in-square cake tin and bake for 40 minutes or until firm to touch. Cool in tin, then cut into 5cm/2in squares and place on a wire rack.

3 To make glaze, place chocolate in a heatproof bowl set over a saucepan of simmering water and heat, stirring, until chocolate melts. Stir in oil. Spoon glaze over brownies and stand until set.

Note: These intensely chocolatey and tender treats will stay moist and delicious for several days if stored in an airtight container in a cool, dry place.

Makes 20

ingredients

1¹/₂ cups/375g/12oz sugar
200g/6¹/₂oz dark chocolate, melted
1 cup/250mL/8fl oz vegetable oil
2 teaspoons vanilla essence
4 eggs
1³/4 cups/220g/7oz flour
1 teaspoon baking powder
<u>Chocolate glaze</u>
185g/6oz dark chocolate
2 teaspoons vegetable oil

Oven temperature 180°C, 350°F, Gas 4

chocky road
biscuits

Photograph on right

Method:
1 *Place butter and sugar in a bowl and beat until light and fluffy. Gradually beat in eggs.*
2 *Sift together flour and cocoa powder. Add flour mixture, milk, chocolate, peanuts and chocolate chips to egg mixture and mix well to combine.*
3 *Drop tablespoons of mixture onto lightly greased baking trays and bake for 10 minutes or until biscuits are cooked. Transfer to wire racks to cool.*
Note: *Marshmallows, peanuts and chocolate chips must be the three most favourite additions to any biscuit designed for kids.*
Makes 36

ingredients

250g/8oz butter, softened
1 cup/170g/5¹/₂oz brown sugar
2 eggs, lightly beaten
3 cups/375g/12oz flour
1 cup/100g/3¹/₂oz cocoa powder
¹/₄ cup/60ml/2fl oz buttermilk or milk
155g/5oz white chocolate, roughly chopped
90g/3oz dry roasted peanuts
185g/6oz chocolate chips

Oven temperature 180°C, 350°F, Gas 4

Method:
1 *Place chocolate in a heatproof bowl set over a saucepan of simmering water and heat, stirring, until smooth. Remove bowl from pan and set aside to cool slightly.*
2 *Place butter and sugar in a bowl and beat until light and fluffy. Add sifted flour, baking powder and chocolate to butter mixture and mix well to combine.*
3 *Roll tablespoons of mixture into balls and place on lightly greased baking trays. Flatten slightly and press a chocolate freckle or a caramel whirl into the centre of each cookie. Bake for 12 minutes or until cookies are firm. Transfer to wire racks to cool.*
Note: *A buttery shortbread-biscuit base is the perfect foil for sweet confectionery decorations.*
Makes 36

crazy
cookies

Photograph on right

ingredients

75g/2¹/₂oz milk chocolate
220g/7oz butter, softened
1 cup/220g/7oz caster sugar
1¹/₂ cups/185g/6oz plain flour
³/₄ teaspoons baking powder
60g/2oz freckles (hundreds-and-thousands-coated chocolates)
60g/2oz caramel whirls

Oven temperature 180°C, 350°F, Gas 4

choc-almond
biscotti

Photograph also appears on Page 7

Method:

1 Sift together flour, cocoa powder and bicarbonate of soda into a bowl. Make a well in the centre of the flour mixture, add sugar, almonds and eggs and mix well to form a soft dough.

2 Turn dough onto a lightly floured surface and knead until smooth. Divide dough into four equal portions. Roll out each portion of dough to make a strip that is 5mm/1/4in thick and 4cm/1 1/2in wide.

3 Place strips on a baking tray lined with nonstick baking paper. Brush with egg yolk and bake for 30 minutes or until lightly browned. Cut strips into 1cm/1/2in slices, return to baking tray and bake for 10 minutes longer or until dry.

Note: Biscuits may be partially dipped into melted chocolate for a two-toned effect. Before the chocolate sets completely, dip into toasted crushed almonds.

Makes 35

ingredients

2 cups/250g/8oz flour
3/4 cup/75g/2 1/2oz cocoa powder
1 teaspoon bicarbonate of soda
1 cup/250g/8oz sugar
200g/6 1/2oz blanched almonds
2 eggs
1 egg yolk

Oven temperature 180°C, 350°F, Gas 4

double-fudge
blondies

Method:

1 To make filling, place cream cheese, chocolate, maple syrup, egg and flour in a bowl and beat until smooth. Set aside.
2 Place butter, sugar and vanilla essence in a bowl and beat until light and fluffy. Gradually beat in eggs.
3 Sift together flour and baking powder over butter mixture. Add chocolate and mix well to combine.
4 Spread half the mixture over the base of a greased and lined 23cm/9in-square cake tin. Top with cream-cheese filling and then with remaining mixture. Bake for 40 minutes or until firm. Cool in tin, then cut into squares.

Note: These lusciously rich white brownies can double as a dinner party dessert if drizzled with melted white or dark chocolate and topped with toasted flaked almonds.

Makes 24

ingredients

250g/8oz butter, softened
1 1/2 cups/375g/12oz sugar
1 teaspoon vanilla essence
4 eggs, lightly beaten
1 3/4 cups/220g/7oz flour
1/2 teaspoon baking powder
185g/6oz white chocolate, melted
<u>Cream-cheese filling</u>
250g/8oz cream cheese, softened
60g/2oz white chocolate, melted
1/4 cup/60mL/2fl oz maple syrup
1 egg
1 tablespoon flour

Oven temperature 180°C, 350°F, Gas 4

night-sky
cookies

Photograph on right

ingredients

125g/4oz butter, softened
³/4 cup/170g/5¹/2oz caster sugar
¹/2 teaspoon almond essence
1 egg, lightly beaten
2 cups/250g/8oz flour
¹/2 teaspoon baking powder
¹/4 cup/60mL/2fl oz milk
125g/4oz dark chocolate, melted
90g/3oz white chocolate, melted

Method:

1 *Place butter, sugar and almond essence in a bowl and beat until light and fluffy. Gradually beat in egg.*
2 *Sift together flour and baking powder. Fold flour mixture and milk, alternately, into butter mixture and mix to form a soft dough.*
3 *Roll out dough on a lightly floured surface to 0.5cm/¹/4in thick. Using a star and a moon-shaped cookie cutter, cut out cookies. Place cookies on lightly greased baking trays and bake for 10 minutes or until cookies are golden and cooked. Transfer to wire racks to cool.*
4 *Dip tops of moon-shaped cookies in white chocolate and tips of star-shaped cookies in dark chocolate. Place on wire racks to set.*

Makes 24

Oven temperature 190°C, 375°F, Gas 5

chocolate
macaroons

Photograph on right

ingredients

2 egg whites
³/4 cup/170g/5¹/2oz caster sugar
¹/2 cup/45g/1¹/2oz cocoa powder, sifted
1¹/2 cups/140g/4¹/2oz shredded coconut

Method:

1 *Place egg whites in a bowl and beat until stiff peaks form. Gradually beat in sugar and continue beating until mixture is thick and glossy.*
2 *Fold cocoa powder and coconut into egg whites. Drop tablespoons of mixture onto greased baking trays and bake for 15 minutes or until macaroons are firm. Transfer to wire racks to cool.*
Note: *Avoid baking these on a humid day as moisture will affect their texture. Store macaroons in an airtight container in a cool, dry place.*

Makes 20

Oven temperature 180°C, 350°F, Gas 4

chocolate-mocha cake

a piece of cake

Whether it be for a tempting snack,

a special treat or a formal afternoon tea, a freshly baked cake is the most universally accepted offering. Try cake cut in wedges with cream, or a rich buttery cake served on its own or with a rich chocolate sauce. The baked delights within this chapter include: cheesecake, torte, mud cake, choc-meringue cake, yoghurt cake, pound cake, gâteau and even Grandma's favourite chocolate cake.

choc-meringue
cake

choc-meringue cake

ingredients

Hazelnut meringue
155g/5oz hazelnuts, ground
2 tablespoons cornflour
1¼ cups 315g sugar
6 egg whites
Chocolate filling
220g/8oz unsalted butter
185g/6oz dark chocolate, melted
3 tablespoons caster sugar
2 cups/500mL/16fl oz cream
2 tablespoons brandy
125g/4oz hazelnuts, ground
Chocolate topping
155g/5oz dark chocolate
2 teaspoon vegetable oil
whipped cream, for decoration

Oven temperature 120°C, 250°F, Gas 1

Method:

1 To make meringue, mix together ground hazelnuts, cornflour and ³/₄ cup/185g sugar. Beat egg whites until soft peaks form, add remaining sugar a little at a time and beat until thick and glossy. Fold into hazelnut mixture.

2 Mark three 20cm/8in squares on baking paper and place on baking trays. Place meringue mixture in a piping bag fitted with a small plain nozzle and pipe mixture to outline squares, then fill squares with piped lines of mixture. Bake for 40-50 minutes, or until crisp and dry.

3 To make filling, beat butter until soft. Add chocolate, caster sugar and cream and beat until thick. Fold in brandy and hazelnuts.

4 To make topping, place chocolate and oil in the top of a double saucepan and heat over simmering water, stirring until chocolate melts and mixture is smooth. Remove top pan and set aside to cool.

5 To assemble cake, place a layer of meringue on a serving plate and spread with half the filling. Top with another meringue layer and remaining filling. Cut remaining meringue into squares and position at angles on top of cake. Drizzle with topping and decorate with cream.

Serves 10

Oven temperature 190°C, 375°F, Gas 5

chocolate
pound cake

Method:

1 Place butter, sugar and vanilla essence in a bowl and beat until light and fluffy. Gradually beat in eggs.
2 Sift together baking powder, flour and cocoa powder. Fold flour mixture and milk, alternately, into butter mixture.
3 Pour mixture into a greased and lined 20cm/8in-square cake tin and bake for 55 minutes or until cake is cooked when tested with a skewer. Stand cake in tin for 10 minutes before turning onto a wire rack to cool.

Note: This rich buttery cake can be served plain, with a readymade chocolate sauce or with cream. A simple glacé icing drizzled over the top makes another delicious alternative.

Makes one 20cm/8in square cake

ingredients

185g/6oz butter, softened
1 1/2 cups/330g/10 1/2oz caster sugar
3 teaspoons vanilla essence
3 eggs, lightly beaten
2 cups/250g/8oz plain flour
2 teaspoons baking powder
1/2 cup/45g/1 1/2oz cocoa powder
1 1/4 cups/315ml/10fl oz milk

grandma's
chocolate cake

Method:

1 *Place butter, caster sugar, eggs and vanilla essence in a bowl and beat until light and fluffy. Sift together baking powder, flour and cocoa powder.*

2 *Fold flour mixture and milk, alternately, into butter mixture. Divide mixture between four greased and lined 2cm/9in-round cake tins and bake for 25 minutes or until cakes are cooked when tested with a skewer. Turn cakes onto wire racks to cool.*

3 *To make filling, place chocolate and butter in a heatproof bowl set over a saucepan of simmering water and heat, stirring, until mixture is smooth. Remove bowl from pan. Add icing sugar and sour cream and mix until smooth.*

4 *To assemble cake, place one cake on a serving plate, spread with some jam and top with some filling. Top with a second cake, some more jam and filling. Repeat layers to use all cakes and jam. Finish with a layer of cake and spread remaining filling over top and sides of cake.*

Makes one 23cm/9in-round cake

ingredients

125g/4oz butter, softened
2 cups/440g/14oz caster sugar
2 eggs
2 teaspoons vanilla essence
1 3/4 cup/215g/7oz plain flour
2 teaspoons baking powder
3/4 cup/75g/2 1/2oz cocoa powder
1 cup/250ml/8fl oz buttermilk
<u>Chocolate sour-cream filling</u>
185g/6oz dark chocolate,
broken into pieces
125g/4oz butter, chopped
3 1/4 cups/500g/1 lb icing sugar, sifted
1/2 cup/125g/4oz sour cream
3/4 cup/235g/7 1/2oz raspberry jam

Oven temperature 180°C, 350°F, Gas 4

23

chocolate-
espresso cheesecake

Photograph on right

Method:

1 To make base, place biscuit crumbs and butter in a bowl and mix to combine. Press mixture over the base of a lightly greased and lined 20cm/8in springform tin. Refrigerate until firm.

2 To make filling, place coffee powder and water in a bowl and mix until coffee powder dissolves. Set aside to cool slightly.

3 Place cream cheese, sour cream, eggs, sugar and coffee mixture in a bowl and beat until smooth.

4 Pour half the filling over prepared base. Drop 4 tablespoons of melted chocolate into filling and swirl with a skewer. Repeat with remaining filling and chocolate and bake for 40 minutes or until cheesecake is firm. Cool in tin.

5 To make glaze, place liqueur and rum into a saucepan and bring to simmering over a medium heat. Simmer, stirring occasionally, until mixture reduces by half. Add chocolate, butter and cream and cook, stirring, until mixture is smooth. Remove pan from heat and set aside until mixture thickens slightly. Spread glaze over cheesecake and allow to set.

Serves 10

ingredients

250g/8oz chocolate wafer biscuits, crushed
155g/5oz butter, melted
Chocolate-espresso filling
2 tablespoons instant espresso coffee powder
1 tablespoon hot water
250g/8oz cream cheese, softened
1 cup/250g/8oz sour cream
3 eggs, lightly beaten
1 cup/250g/8oz sugar
155g/5oz dark chocolate, melted
Coffee liqueur glaze
1/4 cup/60mL/2fl oz coffee-flavoured liqueur
1/4 cup/60mL/2fl oz rum
250g/8oz dark chocolate, broken into pieces
60g/2oz butter
1/2 cup/125mL/4fl oz thickened cream (double)

chocolate-
hazelnut torte

Photograph on right

Method:

1 Place chocolate in a heatproof bowl set over a saucepan of simmering water and heat, stirring, until chocolate melts. Remove bowl from pan and let cool slightly.

2 Place egg yolks and sugar in a bowl and beat until thick and pale. Fold chocolate, hazelnuts and rum into egg mixture.

3 Place egg whites into a clean bowl and beat until stiff peaks form. Fold egg whites into chocolate mixture. Pour mixture into a greased and lined 23cm/9in springform tin and bake for 50 minutes or until cake is cooked when tested with a skewer. Cool cake in tin. Dust cake with icing sugar just prior to serving.

Serves 8

ingredients

250g/8oz dark chocolate, broken into pieces
6 eggs, separated
1 cup/250g/8oz sugar
315g/10oz hazelnuts, toasted and roughly chopped
1 tablespoon rum
icing sugar, sifted

chocolate-pecan
gâteau

Method:
1. Place egg yolks, sugar and brandy in a bowl and beat until thick and pale. Place egg whites in a clean bowl and beat until stiff peaks form. Fold egg whites, pecans and flour into egg yolk mixture.
2. Pour mixture into a lightly greased and lined 23cm/9in springform tin and bake for 40 minutes or until cake is firm. Cool in tin.
3. To make glaze, place chocolate, coffee powder, cream and brandy in a heatproof bowl set over a saucepan of simmering water and heat, stirring, until mixture is smooth. Remove bowl from pan and set aside to cool slightly. Spread glaze over top and sides of cooled cake. Sprinkle pecans over top of cake and press into side of cake. Allow to set before serving.

ingredients

4 eggs, separated
3/4 cup/170g/5³/4oz caster sugar
2 tablespoons brandy
200g/6¹/2oz pecans, roughly chopped
2 tablespoons flour
__Chocolate-brandy glaze__
315g/10oz milk chocolate
2 teaspoons instant coffee powder
¹/3 cup/90mL/3fl oz thickened cream (double)
1 tablespoon brandy
155g/5oz pecans, roughly chopped
Oven temperature 160°C, 325°F, Gas 3

Serves 8

simple
chocolate cake

Method:

1 Place butter, sugar and vanilla essence in a bowl and beat until light and fluffy. Gradually beat in eggs.
2 Sift flour, baking powder, cocoa powder and bicarbonate of soda together into a bowl. Fold flour mixture and milk alternately into egg mixture.
3 Pour mixture into a greased and lined 18cm/7in-square cake tin and bake for 40 minutes or until cake is cooked when tested with a skewer. Stand cake in tin for 5 minutes before turning onto a wire rack to cool.
4 To make icing, place chocolate, butter and cream in a heatproof bowl set over a saucepan of simmering water and heat, stirring constantly, until mixture is smooth. Remove bowl from pan and set aside to cool slightly. Spread top and sides of cake with icing and decorate with gold or silver dragees.

Makes one 18cm/7in-square cake

ingredients

125g/4oz butter, softened
1 cup/250g/8oz sugar
1 teaspoon vanilla essence
2 eggs, lightly beaten
1¼ cups/155g/5oz all purpose flour
1½ teaspoons baking powder
½ cup/45g/1½oz cocoa powder
1 teaspoon bicarbonate of soda
1 cup/250ml/8fl oz milk
gold or silver dragees
<u>Chocolate-butter icing</u>
125g/4oz dark chocolate
60g/2oz butter
¼ cup/60ml/2fl oz thickened cream (double)

Oven temperature 180°C, 350°F, Gas 4

27

white chocolate-
yoghurt cake

Method:

1 Place chocolate in a heatproof bowl set over a saucepan of simmering water and heat, stirring, until smooth. Remove bowl from pan and cool slightly.

2 Place flour, baking powder, sugar, eggs, yogurt and butter in a bowl and beat for 5 minutes or until mixture is smooth. Add melted chocolate and mix well to combine.

3 Pour mixture into a greased 23cm/9in-ring tin and bake for 50 minutes or until cake is cooked when tested with a skewer. Stand cake in tin for 5 minutes before turning onto a wire rack to cool.

4 To make icing, place chocolate and cream in a heatproof bowl set over a saucepan of simmering water and heat, stirring, until mixture is smooth. Spread icing over top and sides of cake.

Makes one 23cm/9in-ring cake

ingredients

**155g/5oz white chocolate,
broken into pieces
2 cups/250g/8oz all purpose flour
2$^{1}/_{4}$ teaspoons baking powder
1 cup/220g/7oz caster sugar
2 eggs, lightly beaten
200g/6$^{1}/_{2}$oz natural yoghurt
45g/1$^{1}/_{2}$oz butter, melted
White chocolate icing
75g/2$^{1}/_{2}$oz white chocolate
1 tablespoon thickened
cream (double)**

Oven temperature 180°C, 350°F, Gas 4

the best
mud cake

Method:

1 Place chocolate, caster sugar and butter in a heatproof bowl set over a saucepan of simmering water and heat, stirring, until mixture is smooth. Remove bowl and set aside to cool slightly. Beat in egg yolks one at a time, beating well after each addition. Fold in flour.

2 Place egg whites in a clean bowl and beat until stiff peaks form. Fold egg whites into chocolate mixture. Pour mixture into a greased 23cm/9in springform tin and bake for 45 minutes or until cake is cooked when tested with a skewer. Cool cake in tin.

3 Just prior to serving dust cake with cocoa powder and icing sugar.

Makes one 23cm/9in-round cake

ingredients

350g/11oz dark chocolate, broken into pieces
3/4 cup/170g/5 1/2oz caster sugar
185g/6oz butter, chopped
5 eggs, separated
1/3 cup/45g/1 1/2oz flour, sifted
cocoa powder, sifted
icing sugar, sifted

devil's
food cake

Method:

1 Combine cocoa powder and water in a small bowl and mix until blended. Set aside to cool. Place butter and vanilla essence in a large mixing bowl and beat until light and fluffy. Gradually add sugar, beating well after each addition until mixture is creamy. Beat in eggs one at a time, beating well after each addition.

2 Sift together flour, cornflour, bicarbonate of soda and salt into a bowl. Fold flour mixture and cocoa mixture alternately into egg mixture.

3 Divide batter between three greased and lined 23cm/9in sandwich tins and bake for 20-25 minutes or until cakes are cooked when tested with a skewer. Stand in tins for 5 minutes before turning onto wire racks to cool completely.

4 To make icing, place butter in a mixing bowl and beat until light and fluffy. Mix in egg, egg yolks and icing sugar. Add chocolate and beat until icing is thick and creamy. Sandwich cakes together using whipped cream then cover top and sides with icing.

Serves 12

ingredients

1cup/100g/3¹/₂ oz cocoa powder
1¹/₂ cups/375mL/12fl oz boiling water
375g/12oz unsalted butter, softened
1 teaspoon vanilla essence
1¹/₂ cups/315g/10oz caster sugar
4 eggs
2¹/₂ cups/315g/10oz flour
¹/₂ cup/60g/2oz cornflour
1 teaspoon bicarbonate of soda
1 teaspoon salt
¹/₂ cup/125mL/4fl oz thickened
double cream , whipped
<u>Chocolate butter icing</u>
250g/8oz butter, softened
1 egg and 2 egg yolks
1 cup/155g/5oz icing sugar, sifted
185g/6oz dark chocolate, melted & cooled

Oven temperature 180°C, 350°F, Gas 4

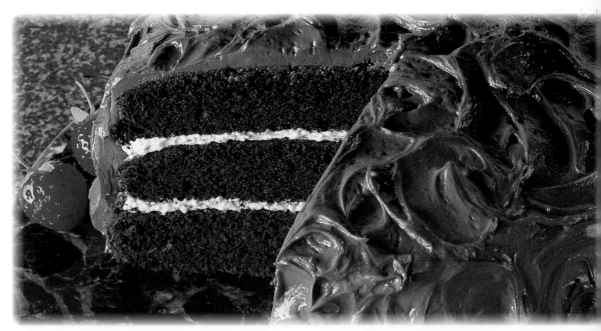

chocolate-
mocha cake

Photograph also appears on page 19

ingredients

**185g/6oz dark chocolate,
broken into small pieces
4 eggs, separated
1/2 cup/110g/31/2oz caster sugar
185g/6oz unsalted butter, softened
and cut into pieces
2 tablespoons strong black coffee
1/2 cup/60g/2oz plain flour, sifted**

Chocolate glaze
**200g/61/2oz dark chocolate,
broken into small pieces
100g/31/2oz unsalted butter
2 tablespoons water**

Method:

1 Place chocolate in top of a double saucepan and heat over simmering water for 5 minutes, or until chocolate melts. Remove top pan from heat and stir until smooth. Set aside to cool.

2 Place egg yolks and sugar in a bowl and beat until pale and fluffy. Add butter and beat mixture until creamy. Add coffee and chocolate and continue beating mixture until creamy. Sift flour over mixture and fold in lightly.

3 Beat egg whites until soft peaks form. Lightly fold egg-white mixture into chocolate mixture. Pour into a greased and lined 20cm/8in-round cake tin and bake for 30 minutes, or until firm to touch. Turn off oven and cool cake in oven with door ajar. Remove from tin and refrigerate for 2 hours or overnight.

4 To make glaze, place chocolate, butter and water in top of a double saucepan and heat over simmering water until chocolate and butter melt. Remove top pan from heat and stir ingredients to combine. Set aside to cool.

5 Remove cake from refrigerator and place on a wire rack. Place on a tray and pour glaze over cake, smoothing it over edges and onto sides with a spatula. Leave until completely set. Transfer cake to a flat serving platter and cut into slices to serve.

Variation: For chocoholics, this cake can be made even more special by making two cakes, then sandwiching them together with whipped cream and decorating the top with chocolate caraques as photographed on page 19.

Serves 8

Oven temperature 160°C, 325°F, Gas 3

31

the best
chocolate torte

the best chocolate torte

ingredients

155g/5oz dark chocolate, broken into pieces
1 cup/170g/5¹/₂oz brown sugar
¹/₂ cup/125ml/4fl oz thickened
cream (double)
2 egg yolks
200g/6¹/₂ oz butter, softened
1 cup/250g/8oz sugar
1 teaspoon vanilla essence
2 eggs, lightly beaten
1¹/₂ teaspoons baking powder
2 cup/250g/8oz cake flour
³/₄ cup/185ml/6fl oz milk
3 egg whites
Rich chocolate icing
³/₄ cup/185g/6oz sugar
³/₄ cup/185ml/6fl oz water
6 egg yolks
200g/6¹/₂oz dark chocolate, melted
250g/8oz butter, chopped
Decorations
90g/3oz flaked almonds, toasted
chocolate-drizzled strawberries

Method:

1 *Place chocolate, brown sugar, cream and egg yolks in a heatproof bowl set over a saucepan of simmering water and cook, stirring constantly, until mixture is smooth. Remove bowl from pan and set aside to cool slightly.*

2 *Place butter, sugar and vanilla essence in a bowl and beat until light and fluffy. Gradually beat in eggs. Sift together flour and baking powder over butter mixture. Add chocolate mixture and milk and mix until well combined.*

3 *Place egg whites in a clean bowl and beat until stiff peaks form. Fold egg whites into chocolate mixture. Pour mixture into two greased and lined 23cm/9in round cake tins and bake for 40 minutes or until cakes are cooked when tested with a skewer. Stand cakes in tins for 5 minutes before turning onto wire racks to cool.*

4 *To make icing, place sugar and water in saucepan and heat over a low heat, stirring constantly, until sugar dissolves. Bring to the boil, then reduce heat and simmer for 4 minutes or until mixture is syrupy.*

5 *Place egg yolks in a bowl and beat until thick and pale. Gradually beat in sugar syrup and melted chocolate. Then gradually beat in butter and continue beating until mixture is thick. Cover and refrigerate until icing is of a spreadable consistency.*

6 *To assemble torte, split each cake horizontally. Place one layer of cake on a serving plate and spread with icing. Top with a second layer of cake and icing. Repeat layers to use remaining cake. Spread top and sides of cake with remaining icing. Press almonds into sides of torte and decorate top with chocolate-drizzled strawberries.*

Note: *To prepare the strawberries, wash, pat dry and place berries on a tray. Pipe thin lines of melted dark or white chocolate back and forth across the strawberries and let stand until set.*

Serves 10-12

hazelnut snowballs

the choc box

Well, if you would like to try your hand

at petits fours, this is the chapter for you. Here are lots of little tidbits to elegantly tantalise the taste buds.

Try truffles, nougat hearts, panforte, tiny cups, little cakes or snowballs— all easy to make and a delight to taste.

pistachio
truffles

Photograph on right

ingredients

**315g/10oz dark chocolate,
broken into pieces
45g/1¹/₂oz butter, chopped
¹/₂ cup/125mL/4fl oz thickened
double cream
2 tablespoons sugar
2 tablespoons Galliano liqueur
125g/4oz chopped pistachio nuts**

Method:
1 *Place chocolate, butter, cream and sugar in a heatproof bowl set over a saucepan of simmering water and heat, stirring, until mixture is smooth. Add liqueur and half the pistachio nuts and mix well to combine. Chill mixture for 1 hour or until firm enough to roll into balls.*
2 *Roll tablespoons of mixture into balls, then roll in remaining pistachio nuts. Chill until required.*
   Note: *To bring out the bright green colour of the pistachios, blanch the shelled nuts in boiling water for 30 seconds, drain and vigorously rub in a clean towel to remove their skins.*
   Serves 4

caramel-
walnut petits fours

Photograph on right

ingredients

**1 cup/250g/8oz sugar
¹/₂ cup/90g/3oz brown sugar
2 cups/500mL/16fl oz thickened
double cream
1 cup/250mL/8fl oz light corn or
golden syrup
60g/2oz butter, chopped
¹/₂ teaspoon bicarbonate of soda
155g/5oz chopped walnuts
1 tablespoon vanilla essence
<u>Chocolate icing</u>
375g/12oz dark or
milk chocolate, melted
2 teaspoons vegetable oil**

Method:
1 *Place sugar, brown sugar, cream, corn or golden syrup and butter in a saucepan and heat over a low heat, stirring constantly, until sugar dissolves. As sugar crystals form on sides of pan, brush with a wet pastry brush.*
2 *Bring syrup to the boil and stir in bicarbonate of soda. Reduce heat and simmer until syrup reaches the hard-ball stage or 120°C/250°F on a sugar thermometer.*
3 *Stir in walnuts and vanilla essence and pour mixture into a greased and foil-lined 20cm/8in -square cake tin. Set aside at room temperature for 5 hours or until caramel sets.*
4 *Remove caramel from tin and cut into 2cm/³/₄in-squares.*
5 *To make icing, combine chocolate and oil. Half dip caramels in melted chocolate, place on greaseproof paper and leave to set.*
   Note: *For easy removal of the caramel from the tin, allow the foil lining to overhang the tin on two opposite sides to form handles for lifting.*
   Makes 40

chocolate
nougat hearts

Method:

1 Place chocolate, butter and cream in a heatproof bowl set over a saucepan of simmering water and heat, stirring, until mixture is smooth.

2 Add nougat and almonds and mix well to combine. Pour mixture into a greased and lined 18x28cm/7x11in shallow cake tin. Refrigerate for 2 hours or until set.

3 Using a heart-shaped cutter, cut out hearts from set mixture.

Note: Dip cutter into warm water and dry on a clean towel between each cut to achieve evenly straight edges.

Makes 40

ingredients

375g/12oz milk chocolate, broken into pieces
45g/1½oz butter, chopped
½ cup/125mL/4fl oz thickened double cream
200g/6½oz nougat, chopped
100g/3½oz almonds, toasted & chopped

chocolate
panforte

Method:

1 Place honey and sugar in a small saucepan and heat, stirring constantly, over a low heat until sugar dissolves. Bring to the boil, then reduce heat and simmer, stirring constantly, for 5 minutes or until mixture thickens.

2 Place almonds, hazelnuts, apricots, peaches, mixed peel, flour, cocoa powder and cinnamon in a bowl and mix to combine. Stir in honey syrup. Add chocolate and mix well to combine.

3 Line an 18x2cm/7x11in shallow cake tin with rice paper. Pour mixture into tin and bake for 20 minutes. Turn onto a wire rack to cool, then cut into small pieces.

Makes 32

ingredients

1 cup/250mL/8fl oz liquid honey
1 cup/250g/8oz sugar
250g/8oz almonds, toasted, chopped
250g/8oz hazelnuts, toasted, chopped
125g/4oz glacé apricots, chopped
125g/4oz glacé peaches, chopped
100g/3¹/₂oz candied mixed peel
1¹/₂ cups/185g/6oz flour, sifted
¹/₃ cup/45g/1¹/₂oz cocoa powder, sifted
2 teaspoons ground cinnamon
155g/5oz dark chocolate, melted
rice paper

tiny fudge cakes

Method:

1 Place dark chocolate and butter in a heatproof bowl set over a saucepan of simmering water and heat, stirring, until mixture is smooth. Remove bowl from pan and set aside to cool slightly.

2 Place egg yolks and sugar in a bowl and beat until thick and pale. Fold flour into egg mixture. Add chocolate mixture to egg mixture and stir to combine.

3 Place egg whites into a clean bowl and beat until stiff peaks form. Fold egg whites into chocolate mixture.

4 Spoon mixture into greased mini-cupcake tins or small paper cupcake cases and bake for 10 minutes. Remove cakes from tins and cool on wire racks.

5 To make icing, place white chocolate and cream in a heatproof bowl set over a saucepan of simmering water and heat, stirring, until

ingredients

100g/3¹/₂oz dark chocolate
60g/2oz butter
3 eggs, separated
¹/₂ cup/100g/3¹/₂oz caster sugar
¹/₄ cup/30g/1oz flour, sifted
White chocolate icing
100g/3¹/₂oz white chocolate, chopped
2 tablespoons thickened double cream
sugared violets

mixture is smooth. Remove bowl from pan and set aside until mixture thickens slightly. Spread icing over cakes and decorate with sugared violets.

Makes 20

Oven temperature 180°C, 350°F, Gas 4

tuile cups
with white chocolate

Photograph on right

Method:

1 To make tuiles, place butter, egg whites, milk, flour and sugar in a bowl and beat until smooth.

2 Place 2 teaspoons of mixture on a lightly greased baking tray and spread out to make a 10 cm/4 in round. Repeat with remaining mixture leaving 10cm/4in between each tuile. Sprinkle with almonds and bake for 3-5 minutes or until edges of tuiles are golden. Using a spatula, carefully remove tuiles from trays and place over a small upturned strainer. Press gently to shape, then allow to cool and harden before removing from strainer.

3 To make filling, place chocolate, butter and cream in a heatproof bowl set over a saucepan of simmering water and heat, stirring, until mixture is smooth. Remove bowl from pan and set aside until mixture thickens slightly. Beat mixture until light and thick. Spoon mixture into a piping bag and pipe into tuile cups.

Makes 28

ingredients

125g/4oz butter, melted
4 egg whites
2 tablespoons milk
1 cup/125g/4oz flour
²/₃ cup/140g/4¹/₂oz caster sugar
60g/2oz flaked almonds
White chocolate filling
250g/8oz white chocolate, broken into pieces
60g/2oz butter, chopped
¹/₄ cup/60mL/2fl oz cream (double)

Oven temperature 160°C, 325°F, Gas 3

hazelnut
snowballs

Method:

1 *Place chocolate, butter, cream and liqueur, if using, in a heatproof bowl set over a saucepan of simmering water and heat, stirring, until mixture is smooth. Remove bowl from pan and set aside to cool slightly.*

2 *Stir chocolate mixture until thick and pliable. Roll tablespoons of mixture into balls. Press a hazelnut into the centre of each ball and roll to enclose nut. Roll balls in coconut and refrigerate for 1 hour or until firm.*

Makes 40

ingredients

200g/6¹/₂oz white chocolate, broken into pieces
45g/1¹/₂oz butter, chopped
¹/₄ cup/60mL/2fl oz thickened double cream
1 tablespoon hazelnut-flavoured liqueur (optional)
125g/4oz hazelnuts, toasted with skins removed
60g/2oz desiccated coconut

chocolate-
fig truffles

Method:

1 Place chocolate, butter, cream, corn or golden syrup and cognac or brandy in a heatproof bowl set over a saucepan of simmering water and heat, stirring, until mixture is smooth. Remove bowl from pan.

2 Add figs and slivered almonds to chocolate mixture and mix well to combine. Chill mixture for 1 hour or until firm enough to roll into balls.

3 Take 3 teaspoons of mixture and roll into balls, then roll in flaked almonds. Place on nonstick baking paper and chill until required.

Note: If preferred, chopped soft dried prunes or dates may be used in place of the figs.

Makes 24

ingredients

185g/6oz milk chocolate, broken into pieces
90g/3oz butter, chopped
1/2 cup/125mL/4fl oz thickened double cream
1/4 cup/60mL/2fl oz light corn syrup or golden syrup
1 tablespoon cognac or brandy
75g/2 1/2oz chopped dried figs
45g/1 1/2oz slivered almonds, toasted
60g/2oz flaked almonds, toasted

truffle easter eggs

something special

Without doubt, chocolate is always

acceptable for that special occasion. Make your own and tempt your friends with great special cakes such as black forest gâteau, chocolate mascarpone roulade or a blissful chocolate bombe.

black forest
gâteau

Method:

1 Place chocolate in a heatproof bowl set over a saucepan of simmering water and heat, stirring, until chocolate melts. Remove bowl from pan and set aside to cool slightly.

2 Sift together flour, baking powder, sugar and cocoa powder into a bowl. Add milk, eggs and butter and beat for 5 minutes or until mixture is smooth. Beat in chocolate until mixture is well combined.

3 Pour mixture into a greased, deep 23cm/ 9in-round cake tin and bake for 60 minutes or until cake is cooked when tested with a skewer. Stand cake in tin for 5 minutes before turning onto a wire rack to cool.

4 To make filling, place cream and sugar in a bowl and beat until soft peaks form. Divide cream into two portions. Fold cherries into one portion.

5 To assemble cake, use a serrated edged knife to cut cake into three even layers. Sprinkle each layer with cherry brandy. Place one layer of cake on a serving plate, spread with half the cherry cream and top with a second layer of cake. Spread with remaining cherry cream and top with remaining layer of cake. Spread top and sides of cake with cream. Decorate top of cake with chocolate curls.

Note: For even more sumptuous results, soak the cherries in extra cherry brandy or Kirsch overnight. Reserve a few cherries to decorate the top of the gâteau, then sprinkle all with a dusting of icing sugar just before serving.

Serves 6-8

ingredients

200g/6¹/₂oz dark chocolate, chopped
3 cups/375g/12oz cake flour
2¹/₂ teaspoons baking powder
1 cup/220g/7oz caster sugar
¹/₄ cup/30g/1oz cocoa powder
1¹/₂ cups/375ml/12fl oz milk
3 eggs, lightly beaten
185g/6oz butter, softened
2 tablespoons cherry brandy
chocolate curls
Cherry Cream Filling
2 cups/500ml/16fl oz thickened double cream
¹/₃ cup/75g/2¹/₂ oz caster sugar
440g/14oz canned pitted cherries, well-drained

Oven temperature 180°C, 350°F, Gas 4

chocolate-
mascarpone roulade

Method:

1 *Place chocolate and coffee in a heatproof bowl set over a saucepan of simmering water and heat, stirring, until mixture is smooth. Cool slightly.*

2 *Beat egg yolks until thick and pale. Gradually beat in caster sugar. Fold chocolate mixture and flour into egg yolks.*

3 *Beat egg whites until stiff peaks form. Fold into chocolate mixture. Pour mixture into a greased and lined 26x32cm/10½ x 12¾in Swiss roll tin and bake for 20 minutes or until firm. Cool in tin.*

4 *To make filling, beat mascarpone, icing sugar and brandy in a bowl.*

5 *Turn roulade onto a clean teatowel sprinkled with caster sugar. Spread with chocolate hazelnut spread and half the filling and roll up. Spread with remaining filling and decorate with frosted rose petals.*

Serves 8-10

ingredients

185g/6oz dark chocolate
¼ cup/60ml/2fl oz strong black coffee
5 eggs, separated
½ cup/100g/3½oz caster sugar
2 tablespoons plain flour, sifted
frosted rose petals
<u>**Mascarpone filling**</u>
375g/12oz mascarpone
2 tablespoons icing sugar
2 tablespoons brandy
½ cup/125g/4oz chocolate-hazelnut spread

47

black-and-white

tart

Photograph on right

black-and-white tart

ingredients

Macaroon shell
2 egg whites
1/2 cup/100g/3 1/2oz caster sugar
220g/7oz desiccated coconut
1/4 cup/30g/1oz flour, sifted
Chocolate sour cream filling
2 egg yolks
**3/4 cup/185mL/6fl oz thickened
double cream**
185g/6oz dark chocolate
2 tablespoons cognac or brandy
185g/6oz white chocolate
2/3 cup/155g/5oz sour cream
Raspberry coulis
250g/8oz raspberries
1 tablespoon icing sugar

Oven temperature 180°C, 350°F, Gas 4

Method:

1 *Place egg whites in a bowl and beat until soft peaks form. Gradually beat in caster sugar. Fold in coconut and flour. Press mixture over base and up sides of a greased and lined 23cm/9in round flan tin with a removable base. Bake for 20-25 minutes or until golden. Stand in tin for 5 minutes then remove and place on a wire rack to cool.*

2 *To make filling, place egg yolks and cream in a heatproof bowl set over a saucepan of simmering water and beat until thick and pale. Stir in dark chocolate and cognac or brandy and continue stirring until chocolate melts. Remove bowl from pan and set aside to cool.*

3 *Place white chocolate and sour cream in a heatproof bowl set over a saucepan of simmering water and heat, stirring, until mixture is smooth. Remove bowl from pan and set aside to cool.*

4 *Place alternating spoonfuls of dark and white mixtures in macaroon shell and, using a skewer, swirl mixtures to give a marbled effect. Chill for 2 hours or until filling is firm.*

5 *To make coulis, place raspberries in a food processor or blender and process to make a purée. Press purée through a sieve to remove seeds, then stir in icing sugar. Serve with tart.*
   Note: *This dessert is best served the day it is made as the macaroon shell may absorb too much moisture on standing and lose its crispness.*
Serves 8

truffle
easter eggs

Photograph also appears on page 45

ingredients

Method:

1 Place a spoonful of dark chocolate in a small easter egg mould and use a small paintbrush to evenly coat. Freeze for 2 minutes or until chocolate sets. Repeat with remaining chocolate to make 32 shells.

2 To make filling, place cream in a saucepan and bring to the boil. Remove pan from heat, add milk chocolate and stir until smooth. Stir in golden syrup and chill for 20 minutes or until mixture is thick enough to pipe.

3 Spoon filling into a piping bag fitted with a star-shaped nozzle and pipe filling into chocolate shells.

Note: Eggs can be moulded and filled several hours in advance. Store in a covered container in a cool, dry place.

Truffle easter eggs
125g/4oz dark chocolate, melted
Truffle filling
¹/₂ cup/125mL/4fl oz thickened
double cream
250g/8oz milk chocolate
1 tablespoon golden syrup

Makes 32

ice-cream
christmas pudding

Method:

1 Place ice cream, apricots, cherries, pears, sultanas, raisins and rum in a bowl and mix to combine. Pour into an oiled and lined 6 cup/1.5 litre/2¹⁄₂ pt-capacity pudding basin.

2 Freeze for 3 hours or until firm. To serve, slice pudding and serve with rum custard.

Note: To help unmould the pudding, briefly hold a wram damp teatowel around the outside of the mould. To serve, slice pudding and serve with rum custard.

Serves 8

ingredients

1 litre/1³⁄₄pt chocolate ice cream, softened
125g/4oz glacé apricots, chopped
125g/4oz glacé cherries, chopped
125g/4oz glacé pears, chopped
90g/3oz sultanas
75g/2¹⁄₂oz raisins, chopped
2 tablespoons rum

yule log

Photograph on right

yule log

ingredients

5 eggs, separated
1/4 cup/60g/2oz caster sugar
100g/3 1/2oz dark chocolate,
melted and cooled
2 tablespoons self-raising flour, sifted
2 tablespoons cocoa powder, sifted
chocolate shavings
White chocolate filling
60g/2oz white chocolate
2/3 cup/170mL/5 1/2fl oz thickened
double cream
Chocolate icing
200g/6 1/2oz dark chocolate, melted
60g/2oz butter, melted

Oven temperature 180°C, 350°F, Gas 4

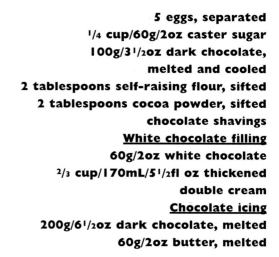

Method:

1 Place egg yolks and sugar in a bowl and beat until thick and pale. Stir in chocolate, flour and cocoa powder.

2 Place egg whites in a clean bowl and beat until stiff peaks form. Fold egg whites into chocolate mixture.

3 Pour mixture into a greased and lined 26x 32cm/10 1/2x12 3/4in-Swiss roll tin and bake for 15 minutes or until firm. Turn cake onto a teatowel sprinkled with caster sugar and roll up from short end. Set aside to cool.

4 To make filling, place white chocolate in a heatproof bowl set over a saucepan of simmering water and heat, stirring, until smooth. Add cream and stir until combined. Cover and chill until thickened and of a spreadable consistency.

5 Unroll cake and spread with filling leaving a 1cm/1/2in border. Re-roll cake.

6 To make icing, combine chocolate and butter and mix until combined. Spread icing over roll then, using a fork, roughly texture the icing. Decorate with chocolate shavings.

Note: Keep this dessert refrigerated until served. Dust log with icing sugar to create 'snow' just before serving.

Serves 8

blissful
chocolate bombe

Method:

1 *To make ice cream, place sugar and egg yolks in a bowl and beat until thick and creamy. Place cream and vanilla bean in a heavy-based saucepan and simmer for 3 minutes. Cool slightly, then remove vanilla bean.*

2 *Gradually add 1 cup/250mL/16fl oz of warm cream to egg mixture, beating well. Add egg mixture to remaining cream, stirring over low heat until mixture coats the back of a spoon. Set aside to cool.*

3 *Stir through cream mixture, pour into a freezerproof tray lined with plastic food wrap, and freeze until almost set. Break up mixture with a fork and place in food processor. Process until mixture is thick and creamy. Pour ice cream into a chilled mould (9 cup/2.25 litre capacity) lined with plastic food wrap. Push a smaller mould, covered with plastic food wrap, into centre of ice cream, forcing ice cream up around the sides of the mould. Freeze until firm.*

4 *To make chocolate mousse, place chocolate and coffee in a bowl and melt over hot water, stirring until smooth. Remove from heat and beat in egg yolks one at a time. Continue beating and add butter and brandy. Allow mixture to cool.*

5 *Beat egg whites until soft peaks form, then beat in sugar. Fold egg whites and cream through chocolate mixture. Remove smaller mould from ice cream. Spoon mousse into centre of ice cream and return to freezer until set.*

Serves 12

ingredients

Vanilla ice cream
1 cup/220g caster sugar
8 egg yolks
2²/₃ cups/660mL/1pt cream
1 vanilla bean
1¹/₂ cups/375mL/12fl oz thickened double cream
Chocolate mousse
175g/5¹/₂oz dark chocolate, chopped
3 tablespoons strong black coffee
4 eggs, separated
15g/¹/₂oz butter, softened
1 tablespoon brandy
3 tablespoons caster sugar
¹/₂ cup/125mL/8fl oz double cream, whipped

pink-and-white
mousse

Method:

1 Place berries in a food processor or blender and process to make a purée. Press purée through a sieve into a saucepan. Stir in $^1/_3$ cup/90g/3oz sugar and liqueur and bring to simmering over a low heat. Simmer, stirring occasionally, until mixture reduces to 1 cup/25mL/8fl oz. Remove pan from heat and set aside.

2 Place water, egg yolks and remaining sugar in a heatproof bowl set over a saucepan of simmering water and beat for 8 minutes or until mixture is light and creamy.
Remove bowl from pan. Add chocolate and vanilla essence and beat until mixture cools. Fold whipped cream into chocolate mixture. Divide mixture into two portions.

3 Stir berry purée into one portion of mixture and leave one portion plain. Drop alternate spoonfuls of berry and plain mixtures into serving glasses. Using a skewer swirl mixtures to give a ripple effect. Refrigerate until firm. Just prior to serving decorate with chocolate curls.

Note: Garnish with additional fresh berries or red and white currants when available.

Serves 8

ingredients

500g/1 lb mixed berries of your choice
1 cup/250g/8oz sugar
1 tablespoon orange-flavoured liqueur
$^1/_4$ cup/60mL/2fl oz water
6 egg yolks
200g/6$^1/_2$oz white chocolate, melted
2 teaspoons vanilla essence
1$^2/_3$ cup/410mL/13fl oz double thickened cream, whipped
white chocolate curls

chocolate ice cream

delightful desserts

The best way to finish off a great meal

is with a delightful dessert. In this chapter we offer some of the most luscious desserts imaginable. From the ultimate chocolate sundae to chocolate self-saucing pudding, you are sure to find something to really delight the taste buds and give your meal the final touch.

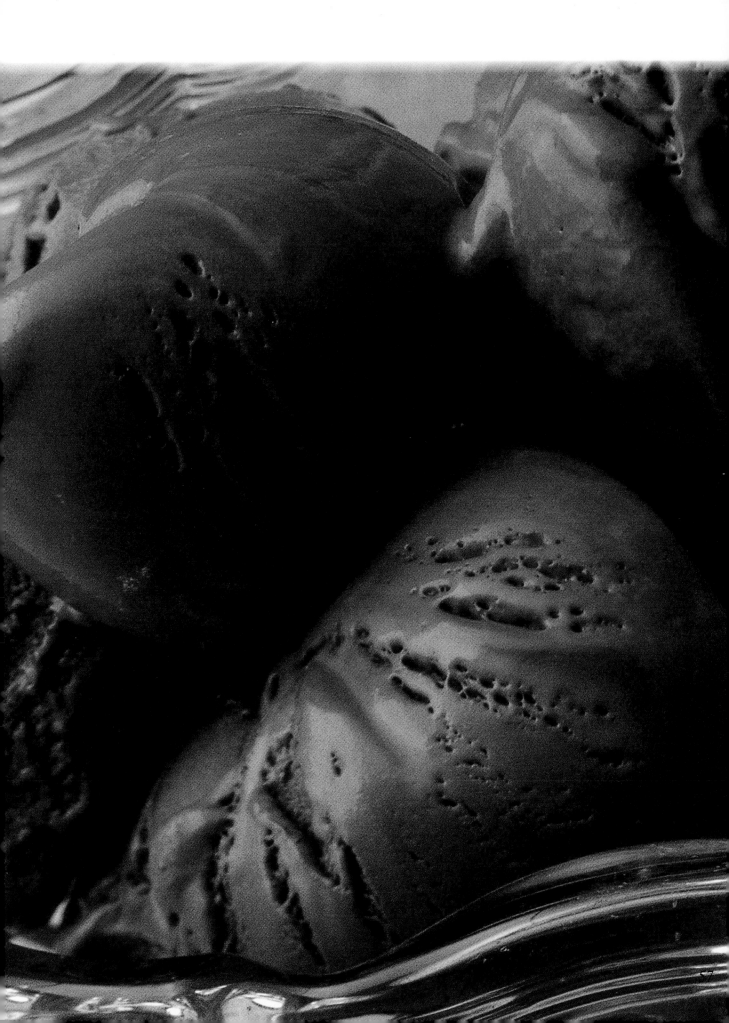

the ultimate
chocolate sundae

Method:

1 To make base, place butter, eggs, caster sugar and vanilla essence in a bowl and beat to combine. Add flour, cocoa powder, dates and pecans and mix well to combine.

2 Pour mixture into a greased and lined 20cm/8in-square cake tin and bake for 30 minutes or until firm to touch, but still fudgey in the centre. Cool in tin, then cut into six squares.

3 To make sauce, place brown sugar, cocoa powder, cream and butter in a saucepan and cook over a low heat, stirring constantly, until sugar dissolves. Bring to the boil, then reduce heat and simmer for 5 minutes or until sauce thickens slightly.

4 To assemble sundaes, top each brownie square with a scoop of vanilla, chocolate and choc-chip ice cream. Drizzle with hot sauce and serve.

Note: Extra fudge sauce can be stored in an airtight container in the refrigerator.

Serves 6

ingredients

6 scoops vanilla ice cream
6 scoops chocolate ice cream
6 scoops choc-chip ice cream
<u>Brownie base</u>
250g/8oz butter, melted
4 eggs, lightly beaten
1¹/₂ cups/330g/10¹/₂oz caster sugar
2 teaspoons vanilla essence
³/₄ cup/90g/3oz flour, sifted
¹/₄ cup/30g/1oz cocoa powder, sifted
60g/2oz chopped dates
45g/1¹/₂oz chopped pecans
<u>Fudge sauce</u>
2 cups/350g/11oz brown sugar
¹/₄ cup/30g/1oz cocoa powder, sifted
1 cup/250mL/8fl oz thickened double cream
2 tablespoons butter

Oven temperature 180°C, 350°F, Gas 4

chocolate
mousse

Method:

1 Place chocolate in a heatproof bowl set over a saucepan of simmering water and heat, stirring, until chocolate melts. Remove bowl from pan and set aside to cool slightly.

2 Gradually beat egg yolks into chocolate. Add butter and beat until smooth. Fold in cream and brandy.

3 Place egg whites into a clean bowl and beat until soft peaks form. Gradually beat in sugar and continue beating until stiff peaks form. Fold egg white mixture into chocolate mixture.

4 Spoon mousse mixture into six dessert glasses and refrigerate until set. Decorate with chocolate curls, if desired.

Note: To make chocolate curls, see instructions on page 76.

Serves 6

ingredients

300g/9¹/₂oz dark chocolate, broken into pieces
4 eggs, separated
100g/3¹/₂oz butter, softened
1 cup/250mL/8fl oz thickened double cream, whipped
1 tablespoon brandy
1 tablespoon sugar
white chocolate curls (optional)

chocolate
ice cream

Photograph also on page 57

Method:
1 *Place sugar and egg yolks in a bowl and beat until thick and pale.*
2 *Place cocoa powder in a saucepan. Gradually stir in milk and cream and heat over a medium heat, stirring constantly, until mixture is almost boiling. Stir in chocolate.*
3 *Remove pan from heat and whisk hot milk mixture into egg mixture. Set aside to cool.*
4 *Pour mixture into a freezerproof container and freeze for 30 minutes or until mixture begins to freeze around edges. Beat mixture until even in texture. Return to freezer and repeat beating process two more times. Freeze until solid. Alternatively, place mixture in an ice-cream maker and freeze according to manufacturer's instructions.*

ingredients

**1 cup/220g/7oz caster sugar
9 egg yolks
¹/₂ cup/45g/1¹/₂oz cocoa powder, sifted
2 cups/500 mL/16fl oz milk
2¹/₂ cups/600mL/1pt thickened
double cream
125g/4oz milk chocolate, melted**

Note: *For true chocoholics, chopped chocolate or chocolate bits can be folded into the mixture before it freezes solid. Serve in scoops with vanilla tuiles or raspberries.*
Serves 8

chocolate
profiteroles

Method:

1 *To make pastry, place water and butter in a saucepan and slowly bring to the boil. As soon as the mixture boils, quickly stir in flour, using a wooden spoon. Cook over a low heat, stirring constantly, for 2 minutes or until mixture is smooth and leaves sides of pan.*

2 *Beat in eggs one at a time, beating well after each addition and until mixture is light and glossy.*

3 *Place heaped tablespoons of mixture on greased baking trays and bake for 10 minutes. Reduce oven temperature to 180°C/350°F/ Gas 4 and cook for 10 minutes longer or until pastries are golden and crisp. Pierce a small hole in the base of each pastry and transfer to wire racks to cool.*

4 *To make filling, place sugar and egg yolks in a bowl and beat until thick and pale. Add flour and beat until combined.*

5 *Place milk, chocolate and liqueur in a saucepan and heat over a medium heat, stirring constantly, until mixture is smooth. Remove pan from heat and slowly stir in egg-yolk mixture. Return pan to heat and cook over medium heat, stirring constantly, until mixture thickens. Remove pan from heat, cover and set aside to cool.*

6 *Place filling in a piping bag fitted with a small, plain nozzle and pipe filling through hole in base of profiteroles. Dip tops of profiteroles in melted chocolate and place on a wire rack to set.*

Note: *Serve with whipped cream and fresh fruit. The pastry puffs can be baked in advance, cooled completely and stored in an airtight container at room temperature overnight or, for longer storage, in the freezer for up to six weeks before filling.*

Serves 6-8

ingredients

185g/6oz dark chocolate, melted
Choux pastry
1 cup/250mL/8fl oz water
90g/3oz butter
1 cup/125g/4oz flour
3 eggs
Chocolate liqueur filling
¹/₂ cup/125g/4oz sugar
3 egg yolks
2 tablespoons flour
1 cup/250mL/8fl oz milk
60g/2oz dark chocolate,
broken into pieces
1 tablespoon orange-flavoured liqueur

Oven temperature 200°C, 400°F, Gas 6

chocolate
soufflé

ingredients

250g/8oz dark chocolate, broken into pieces
1 cup/250mL/8fl oz thickened double cream
6 eggs, separated
1 cup/220g/7oz caster sugar
¼ cup/30g/1oz flour
icing sugar, sifted (optional)

Note: To prepare soufflé dishes, brush interior of each with melted unsalted butter, coating lightly and evenly, then sprinkle lightly with caster sugar to coat.
Serves 6

Method:

1 *Place chocolate and half the cream in a heatproof bowl set over a saucepan of simmering water and heat, stirring constantly, until mixture is smooth. Remove bowl from pan and set aside to cool slightly.*

2 *Place egg yolks and caster sugar in a clean bowl and beat until thick and pale. Gradually beat in flour and remaining cream and beat until combined.*

3 *Transfer egg-yolk mixture to a saucepan and cook over a medium heat, stirring constantly, for 5 minutes or until mixture thickens. Remove pan from heat and stir in chocolate mixture.*

4 *Place egg whites in a clean bowl and beat until stiff peaks form. Fold egg whites into chocolate mixture. Divide mixture evenly between six buttered and sugared 1 cup/250mL/ 8fl oz-capacity soufflé dishes and bake for 25 minutes or until soufflésare puffed. Dust with icing sugar, if desired, and serve immediately.*

sacher torte

Photograph on right

sacher torte

ingredients

250g/8oz butter, softened
1½ cups/265g/8½oz brown sugar
2 teaspoons vanilla essence
2 eggs, lightly beaten
1½ cups/185g/6oz flour
²/3 cup/60g/2oz cocoa powder
³/4 teaspoon baking powder
1½ cups/375mL/8fl oz buttermilk
½ cup/155g/5oz apricot jam
<u>Dark chocolate icing</u>
185g/6oz dark chocolate,
broken into pieces
185g/6oz butter, chopped

Oven temperature 180°C, 350°F, Gas 4

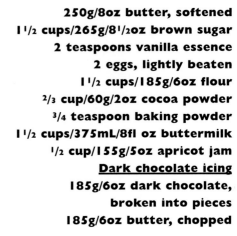

Method:

1 *Place butter, sugar and vanilla essence in a bowl and beat until light and fluffy. Gradually beat in eggs.*
2 *Sift together flour, cocoa powder and baking powder over butter mixture. Add buttermilk and mix well to combine.*
3 *Pour mixture into two greased and lined 23cm/ 9in cake tins and bake for 25 minutes or until cakes are cooked when tested with a skewer. Stand cakes in tins for 5 minutes before turning onto wire racks to cool.*
4 *To make icing, place chocolate and butter in a heatproof bowl set over a saucepan of simmering water and heat, stirring, until mixture is smooth. Remove bowl from pan and set aside to cool until mixture thickens and has a spreadable consistency.*

5 *To assemble cake, place one cake on a serving plate and spread with jam. Top with remaining cake and spread top and sides with icing. Place remaining icing in a piping bag and pipe swirls around edge of cake.*
Note: *This Austrian favourite comes complete with a hidden layer of apricot jam. The words 'Sacher Torte' piped onto the top of the cake in chocolate adds a touch of authenticity to the decoration.*
Serves 8-10

chocolate
self-saucing pudding

Method:

1 Sift together flour, baking powder and cocoa powder in a bowl. Add caster sugar and mix to combine. Make a well in the centre of the dry ingredients, add milk and butter and mix well to combine. Pour mixture into a greased 4 cup/1 litre/1^3/$_4$pt-capacity ovenproof dish.

2 To make sauce, place brown sugar and cocoa powder in a bowl. Gradually add water and mix until smooth. Carefully pour sauce over mixture in dish and bake for 40 minutes or until cake is cooked when tested with a skewer. Serve scoops of pudding with some of the sauce from the base of the dish and top with a scoop of vanilla or chocolate ice cream.

Serves 6

ingredients

1 cup/125g/4oz all purpose flour
^{3}/$_4$ teaspoon baking powder
^{1}/$_4$ cup/30g/1oz cocoa powder
^{3}/$_4$ cup/170g/5^1/$_2$oz caster sugar
^{1}/$_2$ cup/125ml/4fl oz milk
45g/1^1/$_2$oz butter, melted
<u>Chocolate sauce</u>
^{3}/$_4$ cup/125g/4oz brown sugar
^{1}/$_4$ cup/30g/1oz cocoa powder, sifted
1^1/$_4$ cups/315ml/10fl oz hot water

Oven temperature 180°C, 350°F, Gas 4

cassata
alla siciliana

Method:

1 Place eggs in a large mixing bowl and beat until light and fluffy. Gradually add sugar, beating well after each addition until mixture is creamy. Fold in flour and baking powder. Pour batter into a greased and lined 26x32cm/10¹/₂x12³/₄in Swiss roll-tin and bake for 10-12 minutes or until cooked when tested with a skewer. Turn onto a wire rack to cool.

2 To make filling, place sugar and water in a saucepan and cook over a low heat, stirring constantly, until sugar dissolves. Remove from heat and set aside to cool. Place ricotta cheese in a food processor or blender and process until smooth. Transfer to a bowl and mix in sugar syrup, cream, mixed peel, chocolate, cherries and nuts.

3 Line an 11x21cm/4¹/₂x8¹/₂in loaf dish with plastic food wrap. Cut cake into slices and sprinkle with brandy. Line base and sides of prepared dish with cake. Spoon filling into loaf dish and top with a final layer of cake. Cover and freeze until solid.

4 To make topping, place chocolate and butter in a saucepan and cook, stirring, over a low heat until melted and mixture is well blended. Allow to cool slightly.

5 Turn cassata onto a wire rack and cover with topping. Return to freezer until chocolate sets.
Serving Suggestion: Decorate with glacé fruits and serve with whipped cream.

Serves 10

ingredients

4 eggs
¹/₂ cup/100g/3¹/₂oz caster sugar
³/₄ cup/90g/3oz plain flour, sifted
¹/₂ teaspoon baking powder
¹/₃ cup/90ml/3fl oz brandy
<u>**Cassata filling**</u>
¹/₂ cup/125g/4oz sugar
4 teaspoons water
375g/12oz ricotta cheese
¹/₂ cup/125ml/4fl oz thickened double cream, whipped
60g/2oz mixed peel, chopped
100g/3¹/₂oz dark chocolate, finely chopped
60g/2oz glacé cherries, quartered
45g/1¹/₂oz unsalted pistachio nuts, chopped
<u>**Chocolate topping**</u>
315g/10oz dark chocolate
90g/3oz butter

raspberry-choc
truffle cakes

Photograph on right

1

2

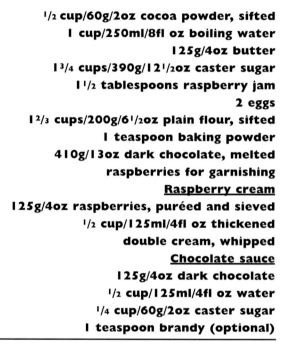

ingredients

1/2 **cup/60g/2oz cocoa powder, sifted**
I **cup/250ml/8fl oz boiling water**
I25g/4oz **butter**
I 3/4 **cups/390g/12 1/2oz caster sugar**
I 1/2 **tablespoons raspberry jam**
2 **eggs**
I 2/3 **cups/200g/6 1/2oz plain flour, sifted**
I **teaspoon baking powder**
4I0g/I3oz **dark chocolate, melted**
raspberries for garnishing
<u>Raspberry cream</u>
I25g/4oz **raspberries, puréed and sieved**
1/2 **cup/I25ml/4fl oz thickened
double cream, whipped**
<u>Chocolate sauce</u>
I25g/4oz **dark chocolate**
1/2 **cup/I25ml/4fl oz water**
1/4 **cup/60g/2oz caster sugar**
I **teaspoon brandy (optional)**

Method:

1 *Combine cocoa powder and boiling water. Mix to dissolve and set aside to cool.*

2 *Place butter, sugar and jam in a bowl and beat until light and fluffy. Beat in eggs one at a time, adding a little flour with each egg. Fold remaining flour, baking powder and cocoa mixture, alternately, into creamed mixture.*

3 *Spoon mixture into eight lightly greased 1/2 cup/125mL/4fl oz capacity ramekins or large muffin tins. Bake for 20-25 minutes or until cakes are cooked when tested with a skewer. Cool for 5 minutes then turn onto wire racks to cool. Turn cakes upside down and scoop out centre leaving a 1cm/1/2in shell. Spread each cake with chocolate to cover top and sides, then place right way up on a wire rack.*

4 *To make cream, fold raspberry purée into cream. Spoon cream into a piping bag fitted with a large nozzle. Carefully turn cakes upside down and pipe in cream to fill cavity. Place right way up on individual serving plates.*

5 *To make sauce, place chocolate and water in a small saucepan and cook over a low heat for 4-5 minutes or until chocolate melts. Add sugar and continue cooking, stirring constantly, until sugar dissolves. Bring just to the boil, then reduce heat and simmer, stirring, for 2 minutes. Set aside to cool for 5 minutes, then stir in brandy, if using. Cool sauce to room temperature.*

To serve: *Decorate plates with sauce.*

Note: *These rich little chocolate cakes filled with a raspberry cream and served with a bittersweet chocolate sauce are a perfect finale to any dinner party. Follow the step-by-step instructions and you will see just how easy this spectacular dessert is.*

Serves 8

frozen maple-
nut parfait

Photograph on right

Method:

1 *Place egg yolks in a bowl and beat until thick and pale. Place sugar and water in a saucepan and heat over a low heat, stirring, until sugar dissolves. Bring mixture to the boil and boil until mixture thickens and reaches soft-ball stage or 118°C/244°F on a sugar thermometer.*

2 *Gradually beat sugar syrup and maple syrup into egg yolks and continue beating until mixture cools. Place cream in a bowl and beat until soft peaks form. Fold cream, macadamia nuts and chocolate into egg mixture.*

3 *Pour mixture into an aluminium foil-lined 15x25cm/6x10in loaf tin and freeze for 5 hours or until firm.*

4 *Turn parfait onto a serving plate, remove foil, cut into slices and drizzle with maple syrup.*
Note: *This light and luscious frozen Italian meringue is the perfect partner for a garnish of fresh fruit and perhaps some almond-flavoured biscotti.*

Serves 8

ingredients

**6 egg yolks
1 cup/220g/7oz caster sugar
1/2 cup/125ml/4fl oz water
1/2 cup/125ml/4fl oz maple syrup
600ml/1pt thickened
double cream
100g/3 1/2oz macadamia nuts,
finely chopped
100g/3 1/2oz white chcolate,
chopped extra maple syrup**

banana
mousse

Photograph on right

Method:

1 *Place gelatine and boiling water in a bowl and stir until gelatine dissolves. Set aside to cool.*

2 *Place bananas, sugar and lemon juice in a food processor and process until smooth. Stir gelatine mixture into banana mixture.*

3 *Place cream and coconut milk in a bowl and beat until soft peaks form. Fold cream mixture into banana mixture.*

4 *Spoon mousse into six serving glasses. Divide melted chocolate between glasses and swirl with a skewer. Refrigerate for 2 hours or until set.*
Note: *When available, dried banana chips make an attractive garnish with fresh mint leaves.*

Serves 6

ingredients

**1 tablespoon powdered gelatine
1/4 cup/60ml/2fl oz boiling water
500g/1 lb ripe bananas
1/4 cup/60g/2oz sugar
1 tablespoon lemon juice
220ml/7fl oz thickened
double cream
100ml/3 1/2fl oz coconut milk
100g/3 1/2oz dark chocolate, melted**

techniques

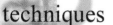

The source of chocolate, the cacao tree, was one of the greatest discoveries made on the American continent. Chocolate's scientific name is Theobroma cacao – theobroma means 'food of the gods'.

Storing chocolate

Chocolate should be stored in a dry, airy place at a temperature of about 16°C/60°F. If stored in unsuitable conditions, the cocoa butter in chocolate may rise to the surface, leaving a white film. A similar discoloration occurs when water condenses on the surface. This often happens to refrigerated chocolates that are too loosely wrapped. Chocolate affected in this way is still suitable for melting, but not for grating.

Melting chocolate

Chocolate melts more rapidly if broken into small pieces. The melting process should occur slowly since chocolate scorches if overheated. To melt chocolate, place the chocolate in the top of a double saucepan or in a bowl set over a saucepan of simmering water and heat, stirring, until chocolate melts and becomes smooth. Alternatively, chocolate can be melted in the microwave. To melt 375g/12oz chocolate, break it into small pieces and place in a microwavable glass or ceramic bowl or jug and cook on HIGH (100%) for 1¹/₂-2 minutes. Stir. If the chocolate is not completely melted cook for 30-45 seconds longer. When melting chocolate in the microwave you should be aware that it holds its shape and it is important to stir it frequently so that it does not burn.

- The container in which the chocolate is being melted should be kept uncovered and completely dry. Covering could cause condensation and just one drop of water will ruin the chocolate.
- Chocolate 'seizes' if it is overheated, or if it comes into contact with water or steam. Seizing results in the chocolate tightening and becoming a thick mass that will not melt. To rescue seized chocolate, stir in a little cream or vegetable oil, until the chocolate becomes smooth again.

Tempering chocolate

Coarsely chop chocolate to be tempered. Also finely grate a few grams/ounces, of unmelted semisweet or bittersweet coating chocolate. You will need 1 tablespoon grated chocolate for every 125g/4oz of coarsely chopped chocolate. Melt chopped chocolate in a dry bowl set over hot water; stir until smooth. Do not allow chocolate to exceed 46°C/115°F – test with an instant read thermometer. Remove bowl from hot water and set firmly on bench (on a towel is best). Gradually stir in grated chocolate, a spoonful at a time, stirring until melted before adding another spoonful. If the dipping chocolate is semisweet or bittersweet, cool to 30-32°C/86-90°F ; if milk chocolate, cool to 28-31°C/83-88°F. Keep temperature at constant temperature by returning it to the warm water, if temperature drops too much mixture will be too thick to coat properly. Similarly, if temperature rises too high above 32°C/90°F, it will have to be retempered.

choc-o-holic

Watchpoints

- *Do not melt chocolate over a direct flame.*
- *The container in which the chocolate is being melted should be kept uncovered and completely dry. Covering could cause condensation and just one drop of water will ruin the chocolate.*
- *Chocolate 'seizes' if it is over-heated, or if it comes into contact with water or steam. Seizing results in the chocolate tightening and becoming a thick mass that will not melt. To rescue seized chocolate, stir in a little cream or vegetable oil, until the chocolate becomes smooth again.*

Compound chocolate

Compound chocolate, also called chocolate coating, is designed to replace couverture chocolate for coating. It can be purchased in block form or as round discs. Both forms are available in milk or dark chocolate. Compound chocolate is made from a vegetable oil base with sugar, milk solids and flavouring. It contains cocoa powder, but not cocoa butter and is easy to melt. It does not require tempering and is the easiest form for beginners to work with.

Chocolate decorations

Compound caraques

Pour melted chocolate over a cool work surface such as marble, ceramic or granite. Spread the chocolate as smoothly as possible, using a flexible metal spatula, in a layer about .15cm/ $^1/_{16}$ in thick; do not leave any holes. If the chocolate is too thick it will not roll. Allow chocolate to set at room temperature. Holding a long sharp knife at a 45° angle, pull gently over the surface of the chocolate to form scrolls.

Chocolate curls and shavings

Chocolate curls are made from chocolate that is at room temperature. To make shavings, chill the chocolate first. Using a vegetable peeler, shave the sides of the chocolate. Curls or shavings will form depending on the temperature of the chocolate.

Chocolate leaves

Use stiff, fresh, non-poisonous leaves such as rose or lemon leaves. Keep as much stem as possible to hold onto. Wash and dry leaves, brush the shiny surface of the leaf with a thin layer of melted, cooled chocolate. Allow to set at room temperature then carefully peel away leaf.

Piping chocolate

Chocolate can be piped into fancy shapes for decorating desserts or cakes. Trace a simple design on a thin piece of paper. Tape a sheet of baking paper to the work surface and slide the drawing under the sheet of paper. Pipe over outline with melted chocolate. Set aside to firm at room temperature, then remove carefully with a metal spatula and use as desired.

Chocolates cases: Quarter-fill mould with melted chocolate and tap to remove any air bubbles. Brush chocolate evenly up sides of mould to make a shell, then freeze for 2 minutes or until set. Larger chocolate cases to hold desserts can also be made in this way using foil-lined individual metal flan tins, brioche or muffin pans as moulds. When set, remove from tins and fill with a dessert filling such as mousse or a flavoured cream.

marbled
shells

ingredients

200g/6¹/₂oz dark chocolate, melted

200g/6¹/₂oz white chocolate, melted

Creamy chocolate filling

200g/6¹/₂oz milk chocolate

¹/₂ cup/125mL/4fl oz thickened double cream

2 tablespoons coffee-flavoured or hazelnut-flavoured liqueur

1

2   3

Method:

1 *To make filling, place milk chocolate, cream and liqueur in a heatproof bowl set over a saucepan of simmering water and heat, stirring, until mixture is smooth. Remove bowl from pan and set aside until mixture cools and thickens.*

2 *Place a teaspoon of dark chocolate and a teaspoon of white chocolate in a shell-shaped chocolate mould. Swirl with a skewer to marble chocolate and using a small brush, brush chocolate evenly over mould. Tap mould gently on work surface to remove any air bubbles. Repeat with remaining chocolate to make 30 moulds. Freeze for 2 minutes or until chocolate sets.*

3 *Place a small spoonful of filling in each chocolate shell. Spoon equal quantities of the remaining dark and white chocolate over filling to fill mould. Using a skewer, carefully swirl chocolate to give marbled effect. Tap mould gently on work surface. Freeze for 3 minutes or until chocolate sets. Tap moulds gently to remove chocolates.*

Note: *Do not overmix the white and dark chocolates or the marbled effect will diminish. Make sure the first coating sets completely before adding the filling so that the first coating does not crack.*

Makes 30

Chocolate leaves

Choose non-poisonous, fresh, stiff leaves with raised veins. Retain as much stem as possible. Wash leaves, then dry well on absorbent kitchen paper. Brush the underside of the leaves with melted chocolate and allow to set at room temperature. When set, carefully peel away leaf. Use one leaf to decorate an individual dessert, or a make a bunch and use to decorate a large dessert or cake.

Piped chocolate decorations

These are quick and easy to make. Trace a simple design onto a sheet of paper. Tape a sheet of baking or greaseproof paper to your work surface and slide the drawings under the paper. Place melted chocolate into a paper or material piping bag and, following the tracings, pipe thin lines. Allow to set at room temperature and then carefully remove, using a metal spatula. If you are not going to use these decorations immediately, store them in an airtight container in a cool place.

Chocolate cases

To make chocolate cases, quarter-fill the mould with melted chocolate and tap to remove any air bubbles. Brush chocolate evenly up sides of mould to make a shell, then freeze for 2 minutes or until set. Larger chocolate cases to hold desserts can also be made in

this way using foil-lined individual metal flan tins, brioche or muffin tins as moulds. When set, remove from tins and fill with dessert filling such as mousse or a flavoured cream.

Chocolate caraques

These are made by spreading a layer of melted chocolate over a marble, granite or ceramic work surface. Allow the chocolate to set at room temperature. Then, holding a metal pastry scraper or a large knife at a 45° angle slowly push it along the work surface away from you to form the chocolate into cylinders. If chocolate shavings form, then it is too cold and it is best to start again.

Chocolate curls or shavings

Chocolate curls are made from chocolate that is at room temperature. To make shavings, chill the chocolate first. Using a vegetable peeler, shave the sides of the chocolate. Whether curls or shavings form depends on the temperature of the chocolate.

Making a paper piping bag

1 Cut a 25cm/10in square of greaseproof paper.

2 Cut square in half digonally to form two triangles.

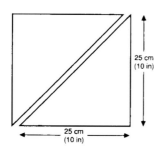

3 To make piping bag, place paper triangles on top of each other and mark the three corners A, B and C.

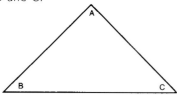

4 Fold corner B around and inside corner A.

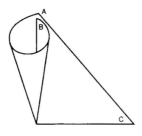

5 Bring corner C around the outside of the bag until it fits exactly behind corner A. At this stage all three corners should be together and point closed.

6 Fold corner A over two or three times to hold the bag together.

7 Snip the point off the bag and drop in icing nozzle. The piping bag can also be used without a nozzle for writing and outlines, in which case only the very tip of the point should be snipped off the bag.

To fill the piping bag: Spoon chocolate or icing into the bag to half fill. Fold the top over about 1cm/^{1}/2 in then fold over again. Fold the tips towards the centre and press with your thumb on the join to force the chocolate or icing out.

Holding the piping bag: To hold the piping bag correctly, grip the bag near the top with the folded or twisted end held between the thumb and fingers. Guide the bag with your free hand. Right-handed people should decorate from left to right, while left-handers will decorate from right to left, the exception being when piping writing.

The appearance of your piping will be directly affected by how you squeeze and relax your grip on the piping bag, that is, the pressure that you apply and the steadiness of that pressure. The pressure should be so consistent that you can move the bag in a free and easy glide with just the right amount of chocolate or icing flowing from the nozzle. A little practice will soon have you feeling confident.

Cooking is not an exact science: one does not require finely calibrated scales, pipettes and scientific equipment to cook, yet the conversion to metric measures in some countries and its interpretations must have intimidated many a good cook.

Weights are given in the recipes only for ingredients such as meats, fish, poultry and some vegetables. Though a few grams/ounces one way or another will not affect the success of your dish.

Though recipes have been tested using the Australian Standard 250mL cup, 20mL tablespoon and 5mL teaspoon, they will work just as well with the US and Canadian 8fl oz cup, or the UK 300mL cup. We have used graduated cup measures in preference to tablespoon measures so that proportions are always the same. Where tablespoon measures have been given, these are not crucial measures, so using the smaller tablespoon of the US or UK will not affect the recipe's success. At least we all agree on the teaspoon size.

For breads, cakes, pastries, etc the only area which might cause concern is where eggs are used, as proportions will then vary. If working with a 250mL or 300mL cup, use large eggs (60g/2oz), adding a little more liquid to the recipe for 300mL cup measures if it seems necessary. Use the medium-sized eggs (55g/1¼oz) with 8fl oz cup measure. A graduated set of measuring cups and spoons is recommended, the cups in particular for measuring dry ingredients. Remember to level such ingredients.

English measures

All measurements are similar to Australian with two exceptions: the English cup measures 300mL/10fl-oz, whereas the Australian cup measure 250mL/8fl ozs. The English tablespoon (the Australian dessertspoon) measures 14.8mL against the Australian tablespoon of 20mL.

American measures

The American reputed pint is 16fl oz, a quart is equal to 32fl oz and the American gallon, 128fl oz. The Imperial measurement is 20fl oz to the pint, 40 fl oz a quart and 160 floz one gallon.

The American tablespoon is equal to 14.8mL, the teaspoon is 5mL. The cup measure is 250mL/8 fl oz, the same as Australia.

Dry measures

All the measures are level, so when you have filled a cup or spoon, level it off with the edge of a knife. The scale below is the "cook's equivalent", it is not an exact conversion of metric to imperial measurement.

The exact metric equivalent is 2.2046lb = 1kg or 1lb = 0.45359kg

Metric		Imperial	
g = grams		oz = ounces	
kg = kilograms		lb = pound	
15g		½oz	
20g		⅔oz	
30g		1oz	
60g		2oz	
90g		3oz	
125g		4oz	¼lb
155g		5oz	
185g		6oz	
220g		7oz	
250g		8oz	½lb
280g		9oz	
315g		10oz	
345g		11oz	
375g		12oz	¾lb
410g		13oz	
440g		14oz	
470g		15oz	
1000g	1kg	35.2oz	2.2lb
	1.5kg		3.3lb

Oven temperatures

The Celsius temperatures given here are not exact; they have been rounded off and are given as a guide only. Follow the manufacturer's temperature guide, relating it to oven description given in the recipe. Remember gas ovens are hottest at the top, electric ovens at the bottom and convection-fan forced ovens are usually even throughout. We included Regulo numbers for gas cookers which may assist. To convert °C to °F multiply °C by 9 and divide by 5 then add 32.

Oven temperatures

	C°	F°	Regulo
Very slow	120	250	1
Slow	150	300	2
Moderately slow	150	325	3
Moderate	180	350	4
Moderately hot	190-200	370-400	5-6
Hot	210-220	410-440	6-7
Very hot	230	450	8
Super hot	250-290	475-500	9-10

Cake dish sizes

Metric	Imperial
15cm	6in
18cm	7in
20cm	8in
23cm	9in

Loaf dish sizes

Metric	Imperial
23x12cm	9x5in
25x8cm	10x3in
28x18cm	11x7in

Liquid measures

Metric	Imperial	Cup & Spoon
mL	fl oz	
millilitres	fluid ounce	
5mL	1/6fl oz	1 teaspoon
20mL	2/3fl oz	1 tablespoon
30mL	1fl oz	1 tablespoon plus 2 teaspoons
60mL	2fl oz	1/4 cup
85mL	2 1/2fl oz	1/3 cup
100mL	3fl oz	3/8 cup
125mL	4fl oz	1/2 cup
150mL	5fl oz	1/4 pint, 1 gill
250mL	8fl oz	1 cup
300mL	10fl oz	1/2 pint)
360mL	12fl oz	1 1/2 cups
420mL	14fl oz	1 3/4 cups
500mL	16fl oz	2 cups
600mL	20fl oz 1 pint,	2 1/2 cups
1 litre	35fl oz 1 3/4 pints,	4 cups

Cup measurements

One cup is equal to the following weights.

	Metric	Imperial
Almonds, flaked	90g	3oz
Almonds, slivered, ground	125g	4oz
Almonds, kernel	155g	5oz
Apples, dried, chopped	125g	4oz
Apricots, dried, chopped	190g	6oz
Breadcrumbs, packet	125g	4oz

	Metric	Imperial
Breadcrumbs, soft	60g	2oz
Cheese, grated	125g	4oz
Choc bits	155g	5oz
Coconut, desiccated	90g	3oz
Cornflakes	30g	1oz
Currants	155g	5oz
Flour	125g	4oz
Fruit, dried (mixed, sultanas etc)	185g	6oz
Ginger, crystallised, glace	250g	8oz
Honey, treacle, golden syrup	315g	10oz
Mixed peel	220g	7oz
Nuts, chopped	125g	4oz
Prunes, chopped	220g	7oz
Rice, cooked	155g	5oz
Rice, uncooked	220g	7oz
Rolled oats	90g	3oz
Sesame seeds	125g	4oz
Shortening (butter, margarine)	250g	8oz
Sugar, brown	155g	5oz
Sugar, granulated or caster	250g	8oz
Sugar, sifted icing	155g	5oz
Wheatgerm	60g	2oz

Length

Some of us are still having trouble converting imperial to metric. In this scale measures have been rounded off to the easiest-to-use and most acceptable figures.

To obtain the exact metric equivalent to convert inches to centimetres, multiply inches by 2.54 Therefore 1 inch equal 25.4 millimetres and 1 millimetre equal 0.03937 inches.

Metric	Imperial
mm=millimetres	in = inches
cm=centimetres	ft = feet
5mm, 0.5cm	1/4in
10mm, 1.0cm	1/2in
20mm, 2.0cm	3/4in
2.5cm	1in
5cm	2in
8cm	3in
10cm	4in
12cm	5in
15cm	6in
18cm	7in
20cm	8in
23cm	9in
25cm	10in
28cm	11in
30cm	1 ft, 12in

index